Marie Hendr

FAST FALLS THE EVENTIDE

Fast Falls the Eventide

*Words for Devotion
and Contemplation*

By
OLLE NYSTEDT

Translated by
CLIFFORD ANSGAR NELSON

AUGUSTANA PRESS
ROCK ISLAND, ILLINOIS

FAST FALLS THE EVENTIDE

CONTENTS

Toward Evening

---

*"Stay with us, for it is toward evening and the
day is now far spent."*   **Luke 24:29**

In the days of our youth, we do not usually give
much thought to the fact that some day evening
will come and the sun will set. And it is only
natural that it should be so. But when one
reaches the sixties, such thoughts arise far more
frequently; evening is approaching. Of course,

I fondly hope that there are still some working hours left. There is yet so much I want to accomplish. But I know quite well that the greater part of the road lies behind me. Sooner or later the shades of night will fall. Ever more frequently now I learn that someone has slipped away. The ranks are thinning. When will my turn come?

In summertime the evenings are long and pleasant. In winter darkness falls soon after midday. When the day of life draws toward its close, circumstances may also be varied. It may resemble a cool evening after an autumn day, when the air is transparent and clear, and the golden yellow leaves begin to fall, one by one. Or it may be like the twilight darkness of late fall, when the north wind snaps the dry branches and the rain-laden skies seem to hang just above the tree tops.

What of the evening of my life? Will there be a long twilight, or will darkness come quickly? Will there be a beautiful sunset, or will it be bitter and drear? I cannot know these things. And I will not be anxious about it, for anxiety avails nothing.

But I will pray: Lord, abide with me! Stay by me during the working hours that still remain, and help me use them well. And when the end of day is come at last, abide with me still, and grant me a blessed journey home!

Abide with me! fast falls the eventide;
The darkness deepens; Lord, with me abide!
When other helpers fail, and comforts flee,
Help of the helpless, O abide with me!

HENRY FRANCIS LYTE

Search Me, O God

Search me, O God, and know my heart!
Try me and know my thoughts!
And see if there be any wicked way in me,
and lead me in the way everlasting!

Psalm 139: 23, 24

The first time a person hears his voice on a record, he is astonished to discover how strange it sounds. He finds it very difficult to recognize it. But if a man has no idea how his own voice sounds, how can he know himself any better in other respects?

It is rather tragic not to know oneself. But actually a man does not know what kind of person he is. It is still more tragic when he imagines that he knows. Someone said: "I'm glad that I have always been a person of good character." Self-satisfaction is the worst kind of blindness. Not even surgery can remove a fault of that kind. Only God can remove it, and sometimes He has to do so by rather severe methods.

Even when we are not completely satisfied with ourselves, we may still be quite blind concerning much that is within us. With the passing of years, we may possibly begin to discover a great deal we formerly failed to perceive. These are seldom v e r y pleasant discoveries. Someone once said that I was selfish. I protested. Now I know that he was right. And now I begin to discern one fault after another—cowardice, dishonesty, a craving for honor, and other ugly things. And then this thought comes to me: How much more is there that I have not yet discovered? What if I am more blind than I imagine?

It is perilous to be blind. A blind man does not know where he is going. Certainly it is needful that we pray God to search our hearts and open our eyes, lest we run the risk of being on the wrong road. That can become very humiliating. But to the humble He gives His grace. It is such He leads on the way everlasting.

Search me, God, and know my heart,
Lord of truth and mercy;
Try me, Thou who from afar
Knowest all my secrets;
And if any wicked way
Should be found within me,
Blessed Saviour, lead Thou me
In the way eternal.

Paraphrase of Psalm 139: 23, 24.

By C. A. WENDELL

He Who Would Enter In

"Behold, I stand at the door and knock."

Revelation 3: 20

An aged woman complained that she had very few friends of her own age. She was 99 years old, so, to be sure, that was not so very strange.

You do not have to be 99 years old to feel alone in the world. Young people, too, may be lonely. But it is especially the lot of many old folks to know loneliness. Time seems to have passed them by. And people also pass by their door. Probably there are very few who step in to greet them. Of course, everyone is so busy.

But even if there is not a single person who takes time to stop at your door, there is still One who says: "Behold, I stand at the door and knock." Perhaps He has stood there a long time without being permitted to come in. But still He stands and waits. Oh, that you might let Him in! He is your best friend.

I know that it is not so easy to open for Him. The house needs to be made clean and orderly, if one shall dare to receive Him. There is so much that is worthless that needs to be thrown out. But who is able to do that? Yes, it is true —if we must wait until everything is as it ought to be, then, doubtless, we shall never be ready.

But He knows exactly how it looks inside. He knows also that we shall never be able to clean and straighten out the house of our hearts. And still He lingers and knocks at the door. For He is eager to come in and to help us make things different. And none other than He can do that, because it involves repentance and forgiveness. That is the only thing that can banish all the old

14

evils and give new life to an old and wretched human heart.

But with him who is willing to receive these gifts, He remains. No longer then need the heart be lonely, for it finds daily companionship with Christ. And that means peace—a peace that passes all understanding. For then He takes on himself all our anxieties and sorrows, and we need no longer carry them alone.

O come today, and do not reckon
Upon the day that is not thine.
The Lord in mercy still doth beckon:
Accept today His grace divine.
Then shall thy prayers and praises rise
A sacred incense to the skies.

F. M. FRANZEN

15

What the Eyes Have Seen

"Mine eyes have seen thy salvation."

Luke 2:30

It was the aged Simeon who uttered these words. His eyes, no doubt, had seen many things, both good and evil. One may wonder if there was not something of continuous searching and seeking in his eyes. He looked for something still, even in the days of old age.

The great day had come for him in the temple.

When he held the baby Jesus in his arms, he said: "Lord, now lettest thou thy servant depart in peace . . . for mine eyes have seen thy salvation." That was what he had been waiting for. Now he had found peace.

People's eyes often reveal what they have witnessed during the years. It leaves its mark in their gaze. That is why the eyes of old folks are so different. Sometimes there is a weary look, and you know that they have seen much trouble and many sorrows. The eyes of others are bitter, and one asks: What have those eyes seen of man's wickedness and the misery of life? Sometimes the eyes of old folks seem to reveal they have seen and learned much that has borne fruit in ripened wisdom. Still other eyes are clear with a look of peace and trustfulness. Perhaps they have seen the salvation of the Lord.

Youthful eyes sparkle with eagerness for adventure. They expect so much. The eyes of the aged no longer anticipate a great deal. Of course, most of life is behind them. But eyes that have seen the salvation of God can still look forward with keen anticipation even when they have grown old. They know that the best is yet to be.

Even when physical eyes grow so dim that glasses help no more, the "inner eye" can see far ahead and behold how the ruddy glow of sunset turns into a golden dawn in that eternal country w h e r e gleams the radiance of a snow-white throne.

How blessed is the vision
E'en here of Thy great love,
But still my spirit yearneth
To see Thy face above,
Where in Thy holy image
I, too, shall join the throng
Of ransomed souls in glory,
And sing the Lamb's new song.

E. E. RYDEN

I Decrease — He Increases

"He must increase, but I must decrease."
John 3:30

It was John the Baptist who spoke thus about Jesus and about himself. It is a humble word which reveals how great a man John was.

I decrease. This is something we must all experience as we grow old. Our powers grow less, our capacities diminish. When we approach 80, it often happens that even our bodies shrivel.

19

One that we remembered as a tall, stately person has become a little old man.

I decrease. Perhaps this becomes an inner experience as well. We come to understand that we are no longer in the stream of things. We find ourselves on the sidelines. There are others who assume responsibility and get things done. It is not very easy to adjust ourselves to such a situation. But that is the way of life, and probably it is wholesome for us. We realize that we are not as indispensable as we thought. Then also we can pause and reflect on our lives, and perhaps discover them in a new perspective. There is much to be ashamed of, so much that we would like to have undone or to have done differently. And what shall we say of all the things that never were accomplished! There is time now to think about it all, and the Spirit of God helps us to see clearly that we have little of merit of which we may boast. We are cut down to size. We decrease.

But how He grows and increases! When a man becomes small, it may be that God grows bigger for him. He that is great in his own eyes gets along pretty well by himself. But when our own bigness shrivels, we need much grace. Then we learn to thank God that He is so abundant in His grace, and that He forgives us and saves us "without any merit or worthiness in me." It is good when a person has learned to understand that it is right that Christ "must increase, but I must decrease."

> *I lay my wants on Jesus,*
> *All fullness dwells in Him;*
> *He heals all my diseases,*
> *He doth my soul redeem.*
> *I lay my griefs on Jesus,*
> *My burdens and my cares;*
> *He from them all releases,*
> *He all my sorrows shares.*
>
> H. BONAR

The Children Go Their Own Ways

My son, keep my words.   Proverbs 7:1

How many fathers and mothers have said just that! And how many have grieved because a son or a daughter has refused to listen!

The relationship between two different generations has always been an occasion for anxiety. The young go their own ways. They do not listen to what we older people say. They think we are old-fashioned and do not understand anything. They, of course, understand everything!

A few decades ago the older folks probably said just about the same concerning us.

It is undoubtedly one of the most bitter experiences of all when parents see their children stray on evil pathways. It does not help to plead with them; nothing helps. The intercessions of many years go unanswered. But do not cease your praying. Never! Remember that you are not alone in your anxiety. The heavenly Father's concern for your child's welfare is still greater than your own. And His arms reach farther than yours.

Even if children do not walk precisely in evil pathways, it still may seem frustrating when we think of them. They go their way; they have other ideas and a different view of life than we. And they just refuse to take any advice.

Yes, it often seems difficult. But the fact that they insist on going their own way should not in itself give us concern. Did we not try to train them in self-reliance? It would not be too desirable to have them become an exact copy of us, would it? And is it really strange that they should look at the world differently than we in many ways? Remember how different life is in countless ways than it was when we were their age! We ought to be careful not to bind them to our own views in a wrong way. Perhaps it is not only the young who need m o r e clarity and breadth in their vision.

Let us not forget that the young, in many ways, have a more difficult time of it than we did in our youth. Let us never be weary in our prayers and intercessions for them.

> *Our children are our greatest care,*
> *A charge which Thou hast given;*
> *In all Thy graces let them share,*
> *And all the joys of heaven.*
> *If a centurion could succeed,*
> *Who for his servant cried,*
> *O grant us faith like his to plead*
> *For those more near allied.*
>
> AUTHOR UNKNOWN

Enjoy Your Money!

"The things you have prepared, whose will they be?" Luke 12:20

It sometimes happens that people become greedy in their old age. They are fearful that their money will not hold out, even though they may be well situated. It may be a sign of senility, a result of growing old. But it may also be that their hearts are set on their possessions, and the closer they approach the grave the more tightly

25

they grasp their money, as though they imagined they could take it with them.

One is tempted to ask them: Who is going to have what you have scraped together? Doubtless they will answer: The children shall have it. But those who have no children, for whom are they gathering?

In most cases, however, it is probably best not to ask that question, because the answer would be: What business is that of yours? But one would fain like to release them from their anxiety over money and help them really to enjoy it.

A rich man who had lost his fortune said: "The only money I have had any pleasure from is what I gave away." Why not have the satisfaction of seeing your money become a blessing?

Perhaps there is a neighbor or a relative who would need some r e l i e f in his poverty and trouble. Why not lift the burden and let some of those greenbacks be a joy both to the giver and the receiver? And consider how much of the work of God's kingdom is hampered for lack of funds. It is surely not God's plan that it should be so. Why not let that money serve God instead of hoarding it—probably for little or no good purpose? Who is going to get what you have saved?

A pastor once said, when he announced the offering in church: "On the last day no one is going to ask how much you left. But perhaps it will be asked: 'How much did you give away while you lived?' "

> *We give Thee but Thine own,*
> *Whate'er the gift may be;*
> *All that we have is Thine alone,*
> *A trust, O Lord, from Thee.*
>
> *To comfort and to bless,*
> *To find a balm for woe,*
> *To tend the lone and fatherless,*
> *Is angels' work below.*
>
> W. W. How

Where You Do Not Wish to Go

"Where you do not wish to go."   John 21:18

Jesus once said to Peter: "When you were young, you girded yourself and walked where you would; but when you are old, you will stretch out your hands, and another will gird you and carry you where you do not wish to go."

All of us may learn how true that is. When we were young, we were free, we cared for ourselves, we went wherever we pleased, and we

28

did whatever we desired. And there was so much we desired.

But gradually we encountered difficulties. Life pushed us into places where we had not intended to go. Things did not turn out as we planned, and we did not reach the goal we had hoped to attain. It is as though someone else had girded us, and brought us where we did not want to go.

It can happen in various ways. It may be that illness has become our companion, and it is a matter of sitting in a chair or lying on a bed. Or business reverses and poverty have come, and life has led us into the shadows. An aged person has to be helped by others. And it is not easy to become dependent on others, not even when they are our own children.

It is saddest of all when sin has gained power over a person and made him its slave. There is no harder master. That tyrant has forced many to go where they did not desire to go.

Jesus has said: "If the Son makes you free, you will be free indeed." He can subdue the devil himself, and liberate the bondservant of sin. To have Jesus Christ as Lord is to be really free.

For when He girds and guides us, we may be sure we are on the right way. Even he who is bound in an external sense may then be free in mind and spirit. A Norwegian bishop who was imprisoned during the war said afterwards: "I have never been so free in my inner spirit as when I was in prison."

> *Make me a captive, Lord,*
> *And then I shall be free;*
> *Force me to render up my sword,*
> *And I shall conqueror be.*
> *I sink in life's alarms*
> *When by myself I stand;*
> *Imprison me within Thine arms*
> *And strong shall be my hand.*
>
> GEORGE MATHESON

Remember to Thank God

Forget not all his benefits.   Psalm 103:2

As the years go by, our thoughts turn more frequently to the past. People, however, not only have varied memories, but also possess powers of recollection in an unequal degree. Some only recall how rugged and difficult life has been. Others remember all the pleasures they have had. Still others remember only the injustices they have suffered and all the wrongs inflicted upon them.

There are also those who revel in the thought of how many good and commendable things they have done, while others feel they have nothing to remember but misfortune and failure.

The more we meditate on the past, the more it leaves its mark on us. He who dwells only on how capable he has been becomes a braggart and proud and even a bit ridiculous. He whose thoughts linger only on past failures and injustices becomes bitter. Both views are unfortunate.

The Psalmist says: "Bless the Lord, O my soul, and forget not all his benefits." The good that God has done—that is really worth remembering. What good we have done ourselves is usually not much to remember. And what evil others have done is best forgotten, for it can only make the heart heavy. But to remember how good God has been to us calls forth songs of joy.

You ask, Can I be sure that I have such good things to remember? Yes, it is quite certain. Ponder a bit, and you will surely discover more blessings than you think. Even you have cause for thanksgiving.

The thankful person is just as happy as the unthankful person is miserable. Ingratitude is like a tight cover on an empty jar; even if it is held under running water, nothing runs into the jar. Gratitude is like an open hand into which God constantly places new gifts.

Forget not all His benefits!

> *O bless the Lord, my soul!*
> *Nor let His mercies lie*
> *Forgotten in unthankfulness,*
> *And without praises die.*
>
> ISAAC WATTS

Earthen Vessels

But we have this treasure in earthen vessels, to show that the transcendent power belongs to God and not to us.   2 Corinthians 4: 7

In the days of our strength, when we are young and healthy and happy in our work, we do not understand too well this word about having our treasure in earthen vessels. We think of the vessel as pretty sound and dependable. It will no doubt survive many a hard knock.

34

But as the years pass by, we shall probably learn that Paul was right. The vessel becomes both chipped and cracked. One flaw after another shows up, both physically and spiritually. We used to be able to do almost anything. Now infirmities are upon us and impede our work. We used to think we were robust and healthy. And we became both hurt and irritated when others failed to appreciate our good qualities. Now we realize that we did not have so much to be proud about. We are rather pitiable creatures. It is a miracle of love that God has been so patient with us. And if we have been of any use in the world, it is only an evidence that the good Lord can make use of rather frail and imperfect tools in His service.

Paul says it is good for us to understand this. Yes, it is God himself who leads us to the place where we realize our own weaknesses, "to show that the transcendent power belongs to God and not to us." The person who has not learned this becomes arrogant and depends on his own power, and that is always insufficient. But he who knows his own weakness understands the more clearly how much he needs help, hence there is room in his life for the power of God. That is why St. Paul could say: "When I am weak, then I am strong." And so it happens that he who in humility has learned how weak he is becomes of greater blessing than when he was so self-sufficient he thought he could do things himself. We have our treasure in earthen vessels. But God's power is made perfect in weakness.

Other refuge have I none;
Hangs my helpless soul on Thee;
Leave, ah, leave me not alone,
Still support and comfort me!
All my trust in Thee is stayed,
All my help from Thee I bring:
Cover my defenseless head
With the shadow of Thy wing.

CHARLES WESLEY

Be Not Anxious

"Therefore . . . do not be anxious."

Matthew 6: 25

It is easy to say that. But for one who is sick or poor or frustrated or has a miserable time of it, it is comparatively difficult to avoid worries. It can sound like mockery to say to such a person: "Do not worry." But Jesus meant what He said.

He did not say it to everybody; only to those

who wanted to be children of the heavenly Father. He who serves Mammon, that is, he who thinks only of himself and how he can get as much as possible for himself, can never cease having anxieties. For such a person has no Father in heaven to count on, but must rely on himself. But God's children need have no worries.

Is that really true? Do the children of God never have any troubles? Of course, they do! But Jesus did not say, "You need not have any troubles." He himself had to suffer much, and to endure a death of anguish. And His followers have often had to do the same. But still He insisted, "You need not have any worries. Your Father is acquainted with your needs."

Just as the Father was with Jesus in Gethsemane and on Golgotha, and wrought blessing and salvation out of all their bitterness, so He also does with your Gethsemane and with all the lesser trials that may come to you. He takes everything into His hand, and it is certain that He knows what you need, which is more than you know yourself. And He gives it to you, too! Therefore, you need not be anxious. You may be sure your Father will never let you go.

It is true that it is not always easy to cast my anxieties on Him and to believe that God is actually blessing me, even when His way is contrary to my will, my feeling, and my reason. But there is something worse than to have things go contrary to my will, and that is to have them go contrary to God's will. For then it will turn out badly, even when everything seems to go well. But if God is permitted to guide me, then all will be well, even when things seem to go ill.

It is not a sign of indifference but of obedience when you let go your anxieties.

> *Thou on the Lord rely*
> *So safe shalt thou go on;*
> *Fix on His work thy steadfast eye,*
> *So shall thy work be done.*
> *No profit canst thou gain*
> *By self-consuming care;*
> *To Him commend thy cause;*
> *His ear attends the softest prayer.*
> PAUL GERHARDT

Persistence in Prayer

Be constant in prayer.   Romans 12:12

We often say, and perhaps not without good cause, that youth finds it hard to be persevering. But persistence in prayer is difficult for older people as well. We would rather get an immediate answer. When it is delayed, we are tempted to give up. It does not seem to be of any avail to pray. And this, in spite of the fact that I have prayed so fervently and gone so regularly to

40

church and read my Bible and tried to keep myself unspotted from the world! In other words, I seem to have a good deal to my credit that God ought to take into account. But perhaps I have too weak a faith. And so I imagine that what is needed is a strong faith to say to God: "Do this and do that, and do it right soon!" But what if God remains silent in order to rid me of the idea that a "strong" faith may claim such merits, and thus I must learn humility? It is only the humble who can receive God's grace.

But it is not so easy humbly to persevere in prayer when God lets us wait—not just a week, or a month, but perhaps years, for an answer. Why does He remain silent? I know I have no right to demand anything of God. And yet He has promised. But now it seems as though He is unwilling.

The story of the Canaanite woman in Matthew 15 has much to teach us at such times. It was she who had to endure those hard words about dogs, but who answered that even the dogs may eat the crumbs that fall from the master's table. In a sermon on this text, Luther writes: "From this Gospel we can learn much concerning our hearts in the time of spiritual trial. As it is in such circumstances, so Christ conducts himself here. During the hour of trial, the heart thinks that God is always saying NO, even when it is not true. Therefore one has to cast such thoughts aside and with a sure trust in God lay hold of God's deep and secret YES over and above His NO, and to confess that His judgment upon us is ever true. And lo! then we have won Him and ensnared Him in His own words, just as the woman ensnared Jesus in His own word."

> *And to this blest assurance*
> *I'll cling for evermore;*
> *And never shall I weary*
> *A Father to implore.*
> *Depart despair and anguish*
> *That oft my soul oppress;*
> *I'll cling to my Saviour*
> *Till He my soul shall bless.*
>
> P. O. NYSTROM

A Conquering Faith

*This is the victory that overcomes the world,
our faith.* 1 John 5: 4

This sentence should be comforting to him who
possesses a strong and dauntless faith. But many
will probably say here: "I dare not make so
great a claim or find assurance from it, for my
faith is no more than a flickering spark." But
note that Jesus has much to say about a small
faith. Faith which is no greater than a mustard
seed is still faith. Our Lord conquered even

43

when He felt himself forsaken by God. His faith was victorious. From Him who is the Master of faith we may take courage and find confidence in our souls. We need not rely on our own little flame of faith. We can put our trust in Him who overcame the world. The strength of such a faith is not that we can summon our own resources to believe, but we can rely on a Lord who keeps His promises. And such a faith is never put to shame. Always it is victorious.

It does not seem true always, does it? How many a soul has not had to struggle to the very end for someone or something, and never been privileged to experience victory. Perhaps he has said, "It is probably because my faith is so weak —it can claim no answer." But still he has continued to pray and wait. Actually, such an attitude reveals a strong faith, even though he may not realize it. And it is such a faith that is victorious, even though the victory is never made manifest in this world.

Jesus himself had to die, forsaken by all. It looked as though His faith had been put to shame. So every one believed. Yet it had overcome the world.

44

Jesus has said: "Blessed are they who have not seen and yet believe." How much more blessed to have been able to see a little, too! But Jesus insists that they who hold fast to God's promises, even when they see no answer to their prayers, are nevertheless blessed. Why? Because some day they shall know that they have not been put to shame. The time will come when the struggles of faith will cease and we shall join instead in thanksgiving to God for His steadfast love and faithfulness.

> *O for a faith that will not shrink,*
> *Tho' pressed by many a foe;*
> *That will not tremble on the brink*
> *Of poverty or woe;*
> *That will not murmur or complain*
> *Beneath the chastening rod,*
> *But in the hour of grief or pain*
> *Can lean upon its God.*
>
> W. H. BATHURST

Nothing Besides Thee

There is nothing upon earth that I desire besides thee. Psalm 73: 25

The man who wrote the 73rd Psalm had a difficult time of it. He felt as though both body and soul were pining away. And he saw how those who cared nothing for God or His will seemed to succeed. Violence and oppression, arrogance and dishonesty, were in the saddle on every side. What was the good of trying to walk in the way

46

of truth and righteousness? He was a lonely man, and he was on the verge of becoming bitter in spirit.

But when he had said these things, he continued: "Nevertheless I am continually with thee." He could not forsake God. However people taunted him, however weary the way, however much he was tempted to give up, he persisted in saying, "Nevertheless, I am continually with thee." In the face of all opposition, he set his defiant "nevertheless."

When he attained this certainty, he found peace. He discovered how all else was of no value compared with possessing God in his heart. "When I have thee, then I ask for nothing else on earth." He could afford to lose all else, but not God. Possessing Him, nothing in life or death could defeat him.

"There is nothing upon earth that I desire besides thee." Who among us dares repeat these words? It is not easy to make them meaningful, so that they have the ring of sincerity and not hypocrisy. How can I endure the thought of losing my home and my loved ones, my work and my health, and many other things of lesser value

47

but which I still "desire" very much? Really, not many of us are mature enough as Christians for this Scripture passage.

But we know that some day both home and loved ones, as well as health and work and everything else, shall be taken from us. It will possibly not happen all at once, but rather bit by bit. But that does not make it any easier. And at last all shall be snatched from us. God grant that in that moment we may possess the assurance to say: "There is nothing upon earth that I desire besides thee."

I know in Whom I trust
When peace and joy forsake me,
When fain my heart would break,
And sorrows overtake me.
The suffering of my Lord,
His anguish, pain, and woe
Remind me of the way
We after Him must go.

J. O. WALLIN

When the Heart Condemns

Whenever our hearts condemn us; . . . God is greater than our hearts, and he knows everything.   1 John 3:20

If our hearts condemn us! Very likely they do so —always. Sometimes we wonder: Is it true of all people that they feel a sense of shame when they look back on their lives, or is it only I who feel that way?

It is ghastly what ugly memories stick with us.

And when I think about it, I see things I have never perceived before. How awfully blind I have been! I must now confess, if I am honest, that basically I imagined that I was pretty good. And now I begin to understand that I have been incredibly selfish all the time. So much pride and uncleanness, so much seeking after honor, so much hypocrisy! Certainly my heart condemns me unceasingly. It cannot be otherwise!

Under such circumstances, we wonder if we have the right to continue reading the sentence —"God is greater than our hearts and he knows everything." But I must believe that, or else there can be no help. Nevertheless, the statement is indeed beyond all measure unreasonable.

God knows everything. What if people knew everything about me! How they would despise me! God knows everything. And He is more stern that anyone else. His judgment is inexorable. And the heart must acknowledge Him to be right.

Then the incomprehensible happens. He is greater than our hearts. When the heart forgave—and it has done so many times—then He judged. But when the heart condemns, then He forgives. Jesus himself has said that. His cross is the seal on God's declaration of acquittal, for it declares that sin is forgiven and guilt is removed.

But the old evil is still with me. I am not clean and unselfish and humble—not yet! My heart still condemns me this very day. My only assurance is this, that God is still greater than my heart, and that He forgives what I have done amiss today.

> There's a wideness in God's mercy,
> Like the wideness of the sea:
> There's a kindness in His justice,
> Which is more than liberty.
> There is welcome for the sinner,
> And more graces for the good;
> There is mercy with the Saviour;
> There is healing in His blood.
>
> F. W. FABER

Patience

Be patient with them all.

1 Thessalonians 5:14

Patience, I suppose, is the kind of courage that is most difficult to reveal. Children seldom have patience, neither do young people, as a rule. Courage they may have in time of danger and when it means wrestling with difficulties. But to have patience is more trying than anything else.

We expect patience from older people. But it

is not certain that it is easy to be patient simply because one is old. That hot, hasty temper still asserts itself. But we ought to have learned something from life. Certain it is we will have need of patience in old age. When illness and aches and pains come, we need fortitude. The same is true when our powers diminish, and we are not able to accomplish as much as before.

"Be patient toward everyone," says our lesson. We are to have a forbearing attitude toward others. And that is not easy.

Young people are so cocksure and overbearing, and they often make us feel we are old, both in ideas and otherwise. I suppose our elders once thought the same about us, even though they were patient and did not say much. Now it is our turn to show patience.

Possibly we are dependent on the help of others, and we feel they are not as accommodating and friendly about it as we might wish. That, of course, is not pleasant. But remember, they are trying to be patient with us. It is always a mutual relationship, and certainly the older person ought to have most of this virtue.

Our New Testament contains many exhortations to patience. In 1 Peter 2:21 the admonition is motivated by the suffering of Christ for us. It is He who has given us the example of patience we should emulate. Here patience is linked with the very heart of our relationship to God. Our Savior had to endure spite, suffering and death for our sake. And think how much patience He has had to reveal toward me through these many years!

And yet, how impatient I become, both in the big and little frustrations of life, and with the people who surround me!

> *When we seek relief*
> *From a longfelt grief,*
> *When temptations come alluring,*
> *Make us patient and enduring,*
> *Show us that bright shore*
> *Where we weep no more!*
>
> N. L. Zinzendorf

He Means All for Our Good

"But God meant it for good."   Genesis 50: 20

It looked pretty hopeless for Joseph when he was sold by his brothers and transported to a foreign land as a slave. But there came a day when he could say to his brothers: "You meant evil against me, but God meant it for good." That which seemed like a most bitter fate for him, God had taken into His hand, and transformed into a blessing.

Suffering always means vexation of spirit. Why should this thing happen to me? Why should I lie here in pain and helplessness, causing so much trouble for others? Why should I have so many reverses and sorrows? The heart often asks such questions in anguish and sometimes in rebellion. And it receives no answer.

There are those who insist that sickness, for example, is the result of lack of faith. They say, "If you believed in God, you would not need to suffer." How superficial! The riddle of suffering will never be solved in this world. But it is apparent that suffering has a mysterious place in God's dealings with us. That does not mean that God always sends suffering. God did not desire that the brothers should treat Joseph that way. But it is a testimony to the almighty power of God that He can use our suffering, even that which comes as a result of the hatred of men, to accomplish His will. We may see this pre-eminently in the suffering of Jesus. It was the power of Satan in the hearts of men that raised the cross. But God has transformed that cross into a symbol of salvation for all ages.

It is depressing to think of the sea of suffering that engulfs the earth. Is there, then, no justice in God's order of things? We find no explanation to help us. Our only recourse is to leave ourselves in God's power in the full assurance that He will make even the evil in this world serve to our advantage. Some day we shall see and know that "God meant it for good."

Ye fearful saints, fresh courage take:
The clouds ye so much dread
Are big with mercy, and shall break
In blessings on your head.
Judge not the Lord by feeble sense,
But trust Him for His grace;
Behind a frowning Providence
He hides a smiling face.

W. COWPER

A Good Soldier

Take your share of suffering as a good soldier of Christ Jesus. 2 Timothy 2: 3

Paul is thinking here, no doubt, of the suffering which young Timothy had to endure as a faithful witness of his Lord Jesus Christ. But may we not apply the same thought to the suffering which many older people are compelled to endure as a result of illness and other trials? He who notes how his strength is diminishing, or how his sight and hearing are failing, or he who lies in bed, broken in health and wracked with pain, can hardly feel that he is much of a soldier. And yet, perhaps, he is fighting a more bitter battle than anything he ever knew in the days of his youth and strength. The temptation to impatience and weariness, even despair, is very great. The heart becomes rebellious. But there is nothing that can be done about it. No one can fight against fate. Is there anything left but silent resignation?

Resignation can be praiseworthy in its stoic heroism. One senses what it has cost. But still— simply to bow before the inevitable is not victory. A soldier does not want to endure hardship unless he become a victor. And it is meant, of course, that a soldier of Christ should gain the victory.

To endure suffering as a good soldier of Jesus Christ means to conquer suffering, so that it may not master the soul, but rather is compelled to serve it. No one can do that by himself. But if we can believe that "God has meant it for good," that He wants the power of His love to be made perfect in our weakness, then there is meaning in all of this. Naturally it is not easy to believe this, because it runs counter to all appearance and reason. It always involves a hard struggle of faith. But in this way many a sick person has borne greater witness to God's power than ever he could have done in time of health. He may not have been aware of it himself, but others, seeing how his sickness made him humble and patient, have sensed that there was an inner power that sustained and helped him to conquer. Soldiers of Christ who do battle on a bed of sickness certainly have an important assignment in the service of the Lord.

> O watch, and fight, and pray,
> The battle ne'er give o'er;
> Renew it boldly every day,
> And help divine implore.
> Ne'er think the victory won,
> Nor lay thine armor down;
> Thine arduous work will not be done
> Till thou receive thy crown.
>
> GEO. HEATH

God Is Faithful

If we are faithless, he remains faithful.

2 Timothy 2: 13

Faithlessness is an ugly word. It touches on our honor and integrity. But can any of us say that we are free entirely from faithlessness?

There was someone—perhaps one who was very near and dear to us—who was in need of help and loving attention, and he did not receive it because we were not aware of his need. We were aware only of our own needs. And how serious have we been about the profession of our Christian faith? Outwardly it s e e m e d fair enough, but how about the heart?

Yes, I have been faithless to people who counted on me, and faithless to God whom I professed to honor and serve.

When a person discovers this and stands exposed in his shame, it becomes a really serious matter. For then all merit and worthiness are gone, and I find that I am a faithless person. How can such a one be saved?

The apostle says: "If we are faithless, he remains faithful." God is not like us. He is faithful. He keeps His word. And Jesus, who is God's Word, has said that he who comes to Him, He will in no wise cast out. For He came to call sinners to himself, not to deal with them according to their merits, but to bring them salvation.

How do I dare believe this? Certainly I cannot know if I have become a better person than I was before. It could easily be a new self-deception if I assume that I am. I have heard of others who have become certain of God's forgiveness and have experienced joy in it. But I am only restless and uneasy.

To this, the answer is that the important thing is not how you feel, but to know that God is faithful to His promise. If you may never trust in your own goodness, no more can you trust in your own feelings. But, despite everything, you are to trust in God's Word. Then you can feel truly assured. For God is faithful and His Word is sure.

I look not inward; that would make me wretched;
For I have naught on which to stay my trust.
Nothing I see save failures and shortcomings,
And weak endeavors, crumbling into dust.

But I look up—into the face of Jesus,
For there my heart can rest, my fears are stilled;
And there is joy, and love, and light for darkness,
And perfect peace, and every hope fulfilled.

ANNIE JOHNSON FLINT

The Lord Will Have Mercy

The Lord will . . . have compassion on his serv-
ants, when he sees that their power is gone.
Deuteronomy 32: 36

It is not a happy discovery to find that our
strength is gone. There is so much to be done,
and I am no longer able to do it. I am old and
spent and good for nothing. I have always
wanted to have a share in the work of God's
kingdom. I have tried to help people, I have

taught Sunday school, I have visited the aged. Now I can no longer do any of these things. Above all, I have been concerned about my family, both in prayer and in other ways. Now it seems I can no longer do even that. It seems inexpressibly sad to be so useless.

For one who feels like that, it is well to ponder this passage: "The Lord will have compassion on his servants, when he sees that their power is gone." The Lord also knows that your power is gone. Yet He does not cast you aside as a worn-out tool, but He will have compassion on you. When a little child is unable to walk farther, its mother does not push it aside, but lifts it up and carries it in her arms. It is so wonderful for a tired little one to rest in mother's arms.

When your strength is gone, God permits you to cast aside all your cares and to rest secure in His arms.

But even this is not easy. Perhaps you are saying, "I will not receive back again the strength that is gone, will I?"

Perhaps not, but in any event, the Lord desires to give you the power to stop complaining and really to help you find release from the many things you have been worrying about, and to let God take care of everything.

To leave one's labors with all their joys and cares, and to rest contented and thankful in the compassion of God—even that you cannot do, unless God gives you the power to do it. But if you accept this power from Him, you will perhaps be able to serve Him just as much as you did in the days of your strength. Remember, God's strength is made perfect in our weakness. So great is His mercy.

Thanksgiving and praise will be the occupation of God's children in heaven. It is important to begin to practice doing that here and now.

E'en down to old age, all My people shall prove
My sovereign, eternal, unchangeable love;
And then, when gray hairs shall their temples adorn
Like lambs they shall still in My bosom be borne.

"K"

That Which Shall Never Pass Away

"Heaven and earth will pass away, but my words will not pass away."   Luke 21: 33

It is often grievous to think of the future. What tragic visitations may yet come upon this earth! It is comforting to begin growing old when the future seems so dark. But our children and our grandchildren—what will they have to endure? It clutches at the heart when we think of them.

Jesus prophesied that the future would bring

difficult days, days when the forces of evil would have great power and create unspeakable misery. It is sometimes said that Jesus, as well as His disciples, had a pessimistic world outlook. But history has proved Him right. Not least of all have these latter times borne witness of it. There are many who now prophesy concerning a final catastrophe. Scientists say that the end of our planet will be destruction, whether through a catastrophe in the universe or through the death of all things by eternal darkness and cold. Then there will be nothing more.

Jesus also tells us that heaven and earth shall pass away. But He adds: "My words shall not pass away." They will remain in the midst of destruction. And when He speaks of the terrible times to come, He says: "When these things begin to take place, look up and raise your heads, because your redemption is drawing near." Catastrophe and destruction are not the end. The pessimists claim they are. But the Kingdom of God will remain when all else shall pass away.

He who belongs to that Kingdom is not promised freedom from tribulation, but he shall be saved f r o m destruction. "For," says Jesus, "your redemption is drawing near." He has a possession which no evil in the world, not even the Evil One, can take from him. Everything on earth is insecure and full of uncertainty. Heaven alone can grant us security.

When we are troubled over the future and tremble at the thought of death, there is no other comfort than this—"The word of our God will stand forever." And He has said of His own: "No one shall snatch them out of my hand."

> In glory He shall come again
> To earth as He ascended;
> So let me wait and watch and pray,
> Until my day is ended.
> That day, O Lord, is hid from me,
> But daily do I wait for Thee.
>
> J. O. WALLIN

They Are Soon Gone

They are soon gone, and we fly away.

Psalm 90:10

When we were young, it sometimes seemed as though time went very slowly. We anticipated one thing or another so eagerly: graduation, promotion, a home of our own. We were anxious to push the calendar ahead.

When we grow old, there is little to wait for except the pension—and the final departure.

70

How long it will be until that day, no one knows. But even if one should become very old, it is still the shorter distance that remains. And time passes so swiftly. It is gone so quickly, as though we flew away. One day I, too, shall be missing, and life will go on—without me.

I still have my work, but soon my task is done. It has gone so swiftly. What have I really accomplished? I still have my loved ones about me, but now and then I wonder how long I shall be with them. I sit at home and gaze at all around me. Every piece of furniture and every knickknack can tell of some event in my life, and perhaps of my parents before me. Soon others will take over everything—perhaps my children or possibly strangers. I hardly feel any longer that I am their real owner, but only their temporary possessor. Everything moves so swiftlyy.

In this psalm the writer prays for divine help so to number his days that he may get a heart of wisdom. I hardly need to be reminded of the brevity of my days, but I do need help to think about it in such a way that I may get a heart of wisdom. Now, it is easy to let such thoughts make one's heart depressed, and perhaps even bitter. But a wise heart seeks anchorage in that which is not transitory but abiding; in that which I need not leave behind me, but may hold fast forever. And that is God's grace. It is something that endures from everlasting to everlasting. My citizenship in heaven is something no one can take from me.

My Jesus as Thou wilt!
All shall be well with me:
Each changing future scene
I gladly trust to Thee.
Thus to my home above
I travel calmly on,
And sing, in life or death,
My Lord, Thy will be done.

BENJAMIN SCHMOLCK

They Who Love His Appearing

To all who have loved his appearing.

2 Timothy 4: 8

Do I belong to those "who have loved his appearing"? The letters of the New Testament contain many passages similar to this. Paul writes that he longs to depart and be with Christ. And among our hymns there are many expressions of this longing for home. "I'm a pilgrim, and I'm a stranger," "We would see Jesus," "I'm but a stranger here," "My heart is yearning ever." But is it? Do I really long for His appearing?

I can easily understand how a very old person, or one who is sick and in great misery, can long to leave this vale of tears for the home of eternal joy. But I am not that old yet, and I am quite comfortable, wherefore I cannot truthfully say that I long for another world. I really want to live a few more years. Is it wrong that I am not eagerly yearning for heaven?

One thing is certain. We should not seek to create any attitudes because we believe them to be proper. Everything that is artificial in its prompting and does not come from the heart is worthless and wrong. And as long as God lets us live, He assuredly wants us to take each day as a gift from His hand and to thank Him for it.

But I know for certain that I am constantly coming nearer the day that will be my last. And that thought does not make me happy. It rather disturbs me. I would like very much to live and to see how my children and my grandchildren will fare. And, honestly, I would like to find joy in life for yet many years to come. And perhaps that need not be considered wrong.

74

But I understand what is implied here. I need to have my relation to God so clear that I need not fear if His summons should come this very day. And I need to have such a certainty concerning "the resurrection of the dead and the life everlasting" that I may experience no uneasiness or fear at the thought of death, but rather possess the assurance that God has prepared something much better for me than this quickly finished life on earth.

Dear Lord, give me a sure faith, so that I may love Thine appearing!

> *I go to heaven, where'er I go,*
> *If Jesus' steps I follow;*
> *The crown of life He will bestow,*
> *When earth this frame shall swallow.*
> *If through this tearful vale*
> *I in that course prevail,*
> *And walk with Jesus here below*
> *I go to heaven, where'er I go.*
>
> H. S. BRORSON

My Savior Is the Judge

"The Father judges no one, but has given all judgment to the Son."   John 5: 22

There are many people, both old and young, who like to dwell on the last things. There are thick volumes that deal with the subject and that seek to set forth exactly when the final day shall be and what will come to pass. One can confidently assert that such books are valueless. Our Bible is very restrained about this matter. Curiosity can find very little there to satisfy it. Jesus declared: "Of that day and that hour no one knows."

But one thing we do know. Jesus has said that our heavenly Father has committed all judgment to His Son. He shall judge us some day. That we know. And that is the most important fact of all.

We also know the character of the Judge. The Gospels make it clear that He judged more sternly than others—more severly than the most exacting judge. He demanded purity, not only in word and deed, but in heart and mind and desire. He said: "You must be perfect."

But at the same time He was more kind and merciful than anyone else. "Neither do I condemn you," He said to the woman who, according to the law, deserved to be stoned to death. He did not quench the smoldering wick. He dealt so gently with shabby souls.

And He was not, as we so often are, sometimes kind and sometimes stern. Rather, He was both at the same time. It was the divine in Him, an indissoluble blending of divine severity and divine mercy.

He it is who will judge us some day. And He is the same yesterday and today and forever. That is why we can be sure that the final judgment will be much more severe and, at the same time, infinitely more merciful than we ever thought. How this will come to pass we cannot know, just as little as anyone could have been able to foresee how, when He was here on earth, He would unite divine severity and divine mercy by dying on the Cross.

May we here and now place ourselves under His severe and yet merciful judgment, that we may thus be ready for the final judgment.

> *O Christ, my Intercessor be,*
> *And for Thy death and merit*
> *Declare my name from judgment free,*
> *With all who life inherit;*
> *That with my brethren I may stand*
> *With Thee in heaven, our fatherland,*
> *Which Thou for us hast purchased.*
>
> B. RINGWALDT

The New Song

And I heard a voice from heaven like the sound of many waters and like the sound of loud thunder; the voice I heard was like the sound of harpers playing on their harps, and they sing a new song before the throne and before the four living creatures and before the elders. No one could learn that song except the hundred and forty-four thousand who had been redeemed from the earth.

Revelation 14: 2, 3

Here on earth the song of God's congregation has often moved into a minor key, reflecting the struggle and tribulation the Lord's faithful have had to endure. But the basic note, nevertheless, has always been praise and thanksgiving. In God's heaven it will sound forth in fullness of joy. There all will become new. And the song of thanksgiving also will be new. God grant that we, too, may sing that song.

Observe what the seer says: "No one could learn that song except those redeemed from the earth." Something must happen to us if we are to be able in due time to sing the song of heaven. We must be redeemed from the earth. Otherwise we are prisoners of earth. We are not free. The human heart so easily becomes fixed on one thing or another—on troubles and sorrows, on possessions and pleasures, on the praises of men. And then it is about these things the heart sings its secret song, and the music of heaven becomes a strange sound that strikes no echo in the soul. That is when we need to be freed, redeemed from earth.

It is impossible to sing two songs at the same time. And still we often try it. We try to sing the song about ourselves and our own things, and the song about God and His Kingdom at the same time. In that case, it will probably result in a song that tells how well we have provided for ourselves and how much we have retained, while still remaining on good terms with God.

How shall we be able to sing the song of the redeemed if He has not been permitted to save us from ourselves, so that we really have something to sing about, something that fills the heart, and for which it must be thankful?

It is rather sad to be centered in oneself and in the things of earth. But it is great riches to possess a free soul that can lift itself to heaven with prayer and praise and thanksgiving. There, in heaven, the song of praise will be new and full and complete!

And when the strife is fierce, the warfare long,
Steals on the earth the distant triumph-song,
And hearts are brave again, and arms are strong.
  Alleluia!
From earth's remotest bounds, from ocean's farthest
  coast,
Through gates of pearl streams in the countless host,
Singing to Father, Son and Holy Ghost. Alleluia!

W. W. How

81

The Resurrection and the Life

*Jesus said: "I am the resurrection and the life;
he who believes in me, though he die, yet shall
he live."*   John 11: 25

How can we become certain of this truth? There
are no real evidences to be had. Many say that
beyond death there is nothing. Faith in the resurrection of the dead and the life everlasting could
possibly be only wishful thinking! The heart becomes troubled by the invasion of such doubts.

However, these things undoubtedly belong to the struggle of faith from which there is no escape.

But it would indeed be rather strange if God —concerning whom we likewise can offer no infallible "proofs"—should have created us with the need of salvation and a yearning for eternity if there were no reality to satisfy our longings. And the soul's rest in God, of which Augustine speaks, would be quite meaningless if it were concerned only with a few short years and ended with death. Truly everything would then lack meaning.

Ultimately our faith in the resurrection of the dead and the life everlasting is a matter of our faith in the trustworthiness of Jesus Christ. It is He who has said: "He who believes in me, though he die, yet shall he live." We have no other evidence than that. But if ever there has been one on this earth whose words are unconditionally reliable and if ever there has been one who has known about the things of God's Kingdom, it surely is He.

And He has offered himself as the guarantor of life eternal. "I am the resurrection and the life." With divine authority He speaks these words. "He who believes in me, though he die, yet shall he live." Faith in Him is the same as fellowship with Him; it is to become partaker of a new kind of life in Him—life eternal. And this is not something that lasts a few years and then comes to an end. It is a life that belongs to a plane that is higher than the one where the laws of mortality hold sway. Death has no significance in that realm.

Everything in this world is uncertain and insecure. But concerning the resurrection from the dead and the life eternal we have the word and promise of Jesus. And that is most certainly true.

> *In Him I have salvation's way discovered*
> *The heritage for me He has recovered.*
> *Though death o'ertakes me,*
> *Christ ne'er forsakes me,*
> *To everlasting life He surely wakes me.*
>
> E. ANDERSDOTTER

To Be With Christ

My desire is to depart and be with Christ.
Philippians 1:23

Sometimes we hear people say: "Since my husband died, or since my wife left me, I am so lonely I could wish to follow and be reunited with my beloved." Or: "Since I lost my child, I have also lost all joy in life. Now I have only one desire—to see my child again." St. Paul's words have been changed to mean: "I am eager

85

to depart and be with my husband, my wife, my child."

We can understand that feeling very well. And certainly, we may pray and hope that God will permit us to see our dear ones again. But it is dangerous to forget what for Paul was the greatest and most important of all—to be with Christ. It is not the companionship of our dear ones, however precious it may be to us, that makes us partakers of eternal life; only fellowship with Christ can do that. It is He who is the resurrection and the life.

When the thought of our departed loved ones comes first, we may be tempted even now to try devious methods of communication with the dead and of seeking to penetrate behind the veil that hides the realm of eternity. That is always hazardous, for then we leave the solid ground of God's Word and enter the dream world of pure human fantasy. When that happens, the danger of pushing Christ aside is great.

Preparation for eternity consists, not in trying to break through the mystery of the eternal realm, but in seeking a living fellowship with Christ, our Savior. That fellowship must begin here, and it will prepare us for heaven by making Jesus Christ our best friend. It is He whom we must thank for all—forgiveness of sins, adoption as sons, and peace with God—and when we come to realize this, we shall begin to understand why it will be heaven just to be with Him forever.

> *Nearer, still nearer, while life shall last,*
> *Till safe in glory my anchor is cast;*
> *Through endless ages ever to be*
> *Nearer, my Saviour, still nearer to Thee.*
>
> C. H. MORRIS

Written in Heaven

"Rejoice that your names are written in heaven."   Luke 10:20

Our names are written somewhere in the parish records of a Christian church. That means that our spiritual home is there. That is a great privilege. It brings us many blessings in the Church of God.

But some day, soon or late, our names will be removed from the rolls, and inscribed in the records of the deceased. Then the question will be, do we have citizenship anywhere else?

Jesus says that we do. He tells us that our names are written in heaven. That means that we have citizenship there.

Can I be sure of that? Yes, absolutely sure!

But I have not been the kind of person I ought to have been. I have not sought God as I ought. I have many ugly things on my conscience. I am a f r a i d that my name has been blotted out up there long ago.

Not so. Your name shall never be removed up there, never in all eternity. For it has been recorded there with the blood of Jesus, and that can never be blotted out. It is not because you have been so godly that it is written there. Nor will it be removed because you have been so ungodly. It was written there only because God loved you. And He still loves you, no matter how strange it may sound. You still have citizenship in heaven.

The danger is that you forget it and do not make use of your right. If you turn away from God and choose another destiny, He will never force you into heaven.

But if you begin to feel alone and homeless, and if your desolate soul knows not where to turn, remember where your name is written. There you will find a welcome. And forgiveness is there for the prodigal son. This is absolutely certain, for your name is written in God's book. Jesus said that this is the greatest cause of rejoicing in all the world.

In Jesus' heart there's room, I know,
And in His heaven of bliss.
He in His gospel tells me so,
Thanks be to God for this.

L. S. BERG

No More Tears

"He will wipe away every tear from their eyes, and death shall be no more, neither shall there be mourning nor crying nor pain any more, for the former things have passed away."

Revelation 21: 4

What these former things are, we know. The seer has recounted them: sorrow, crying, pain, and death. All of us have shared these things: the sorrows that others have caused us, the sorrows that we have made for ourselves by sin and selfishness; sickness, failures, loneliness, and the shadow of death across our pathway. Some day all these things shall be no more. They shall belong to the past. As a mother wipes away the tears of her child and all is well, so God will comfort His children in that day.

All that here has seemed so mysterious and meaningless shall then be explained. All the puzzling questions that have haunted us through life shall find their answer. Then we shall understand that God has a purpose even in the most grievous of our experiences. He is working out the pattern of His love even in the things that caused us tears and sorrow. And we shall thank Him for everything. Heaven will resound with songs of praise. May God help us confidently to trust in this, and rejoice in the hope of such a future.

No one can conceive what God has prepared for His children, writes the apostle. He is "able to do far more abundantly than all that we ask or think." But we may rejoice already in anticipation of it all. Just as young people away from home are made glad at the thought of going home for Christmas, so the children of God may rejoice over the home that awaits them above. And should not this help them to be faithful in their calling and patient in suffering? Trials endure only a little while. After that they shall be no more. But the joy will remain forever!

Thus the ruddy glow of sunset becomes the golden radiance of dawn. The river of death may be chill and cold, but on the other shore the sun is shining, and there is my Lord and Savior standing with open arms to welcome a poor sinner who, in spite of everything, has come home—home for ever!

O precious thought! Some day the mist shall vanish;
Some day the web of gloom shall be unspun.
A day shall break whose beams the night shall banish,
For Christ, the Lamb, shall shine, the glorious Sun.

C. O. ROSENIUS

I Am Coming Soon

"Surely I am coming soon." Amen. Come,
Lord Jesus.   Revelation 22: 20

Sometimes I seem to hear a low, gentle voice
speaking in my ear: "I am coming soon." I grow
uneasy then. For I am not yet ready. I am en-
vious of those who can rejoice when they hear
that voice and are ready to answer: "Amen.
Come, Lord Jesus." There is so much that still

ties me to earth, so much for which I am both ashamed and thankful. May God free me from all that is not from Him, and may He so teach me, when the final summons comes, that I may be able to say of all I possess: "The Lord gave, and the Lord has taken away; blessed be the name of the Lord."

"I am coming soon!" The voice is so friendly. To think that He can speak so kindly to such a one as I! But it is serious, too. Of course, I understand why. And I tremble because of it. Will He ever be able to control me completely? I ought to have my mind fixed on heavenly things, and it is not. The old sinful self in me is still very much alive. And it must die, if I am to live with Christ some day. God be merciful to me!

"I am coming soon!" I am thankful for that voice. When I hear it, I understand better than before the difference between that which is important and what is not so important. And then I sense, as it were, a new kind of thankfulness to God for all He has given to me: my loved ones, my home, my work and all the rest of the lovely joys of life. It is all so undeserved. Of course, it will be hard to leave my dear ones, but I know they are in God's hand. And the parting will be for only a little while.

"I am coming soon!" How incredibly great is not the grace of God! When I look back, I can only blush at everything that is my own, while I marvel over all the goodness of God that I have not deserved. And now my Savior offers to take me by the hand, unworthy as I am, and turn my gaze forward toward eternity. He gives me time for preparation. May I use it aright! He tells me that death is His servant whom I need not fear, and that He has prepared a place for me in heaven.

"Surely, I am coming soon!" Lord, grant that my heart may answer: "Amen. Come, Lord Jesus!"

'Tis but a little while
And He shall come again,
Who died that we might live, who lives
That we with Him may reign:
Then, O my Lord, prepare
My soul for that glad day;
O wash me in Thy precious blood,
And take my sins away!

H. BONAR